MW01705861

Should Know About the RCIA

Charlene Altemose, MSC

Liguori
ONE LIGUORI DRIVE
LIGUORI MO 63057-9999

Imprimi Potest:
Richard Thibodeau, C.Ss.R.
Provincial, Denver Province
The Redemptorists

Imprimatur:
Most Reverend Michael J. Sheridan
Auxiliary Bishop, Archdiocese of St. Louis

ISBN 0-7648-0401-4

© 1999, Charlene Altemose, MSC
Printed in the United States of America
99 00 01 02 03 5 4 3 2 1

All rights reserved. No part of this booklet may be reproduced, stored in a retrieval system, or transmitted without the written permission of Liguori Publications.

Scripture quotations are from the *New Revised Standard Version of the Bible*, copyright © 1989 by the Division of Christian Education of the National Council of the Churches of Christ in the USA. Used with permission. All rights reserved.

To order, call 1-800-325-9521
http://www.liguori.org

Cover design by Ross M. Sherman
Cover photo by Jim Whitmer

Contents

Prayer for the RCIA

O God, we thank you for implanting
the gift of faith in human hearts.
We thank you for sending Jesus, your Son,
as the fullness of your love. May his life and
mission lead us to share in your divine life.

Today we ask you to bless in a special way
all inquirers, catechumens, and candidates,
who have generously responded to the
invitation of Jesus: "Come, follow me."
Help them to persevere in their journey
of faith despite any difficulties.
Bless all those who minister
through the RCIA program so that,
under the guidance of your Holy Spirit,
they may lead others to a life of faith in Jesus
Christ. Grant that all parishioners will take
an active role in bringing new members
into the Church. Call us all to a renewal
of our faith, and inspire us all
to be your light in the world.

Introduction

Lisa curiously opened a letter addressed to her from her husband's parish. It read:

Dear Friend,

According to our records, members of your family are registered in our parish. We not only serve our parishioners, but we also are concerned about their families. Perhaps you wonder at times why we do what we do as Catholics. Or perhaps you have considered becoming a Catholic but just don't know how.

In either case, we invite you to enrich yourself and learn more about Catholics. The ***RCIA (Rite of Christian Initiation of Adults)*** *is for people who want either to learn about Catholics or to become Catholic. If you are in an interfaith marriage and are already actively involved in a church of a different denomination, you may want to understand your family's Catholic faith better. If you are not connected to any faith community, you are most welcome to inquire with us. If after preparation you decide to become Catholic, you will be formally accepted in a solemn celebration at Easter.*

We invite you to explore this opportunity by coming to our RCIA sessions, which meet on Thursday evenings beginning in September. If you have any questions or would like further information, please contact the parish office.

With cordial greetings,
Father Tom

Delighted to receive this invitation, Lisa put the letter aside. She had thought of becoming Catholic because she saw how much the faith meant to her family. The letter was an answer to her secret wish.

There are many "Lisas" who are searching for a way to help them meet their spiritual needs and identify with a **community of faith**. People who feel the desire to know more about the Catholic Church and to explore its life more may simply need a friendly invitation. The RCIA is the Church's way of extending such an invitation.

But what is the RCIA? How does it operate? What are the steps in the process? What is needed for the RCIA to be successful in a parish? The answers to these and many other questions are in this booklet, a basic tool of information for Catholics or others who hear of the RCIA and may wonder what it entails. This booklet also can be very useful to those directly involved in a parish RCIA program.

Editor's Note: First occurrences of special terms are set in boldface type. They are defined in "RCIA Terms," page 40.

PART I

What Is the RCIA?

Religion—Rooted in Our Cultural Heritage

Before we explain the RCIA process, it is helpful to explore how human beings understand the way God directs us in our quest for meaning. Each person's journey of faith is unique.

Look into your own life. How did you first find out about God? How did you come to know God and to practice religion? What factors have helped you shape your image of God? How have you come to express your faith?

You were born at a specific time into a specific culture, with its unique outlook and value system. Besides being given physical life, you also have inherited a certain attitude toward life from your parents and surroundings. But as you grow older you develop your unique response to life, including the religion you follow.

Many practice throughout life the religion with which they were raised. Others may not have a place for religion in their lives, while still others, through personal searching, choose to change to a different religion. The RCIA is directed to those who are searching and inquiring about the Catholic way of life.

Evangelization—Catholics Leading Others Into the Church

Before a parish RCIA program can become a compelling means for persons to enter the Church, Catholics need to create a welcoming community within the parish. It is in the parish that we uniquely experience Church and live out the Catholic commitment.

The RCIA cannot operate effectively without the dedication and determination of Catholics who are convinced that the Catholic way of life has enabled them to develop a deep relationship with the Lord. Only through the **witness** of Catholics and the sharing of their faith experience can those who are searching come to understand what Catholicism means. They are attracted to the Catholic way of life mainly by the example they see in others.

Although our Sunday liturgical celebration and worship is the focal point of our Catholic faith, we must do more to be considered a practicing and witnessing Catholic. Our faith follows us throughout our work week into our daily lives. Each day calls us to live our faith fully.

The example, witness, and sharing of the Catholic way of life with those who are searching is **evangelization**. To evangelize is to live in such a way that people are attracted to the Catholic faith and wish to be part of it. Ask anyone who has come into the Church what motivated them. It's been my personal experience that most people respond to the question, "Why do you want to become Catholic?" by saying "Because of the way Catholics I know live their faith and because of how much it means to them."

Specific Ways Catholics Can Evangelize

Here are some specific ways Catholics can effectively draw others to Catholicism directly or indirectly, perhaps without even realizing that they are evangelizers.

- Be aware that everyone each day is called to **conversion**. Even long-time Catholics have an ongoing responsibility to regularly examine their relationship to God, others, and themselves and to pray for the grace to improve these relationships.

- Know what the Catholic faith teaches. Be knowledgeable about what it means to be Catholic. Keeping abreast of the ways our Catholic life is lived and what the Church teaches in our post-Vatican II era is a life-long learning process. By being knowledgeable in the faith, you encourage others to ask questions and seek answers.

- Be at ease in talking about the way the Lord touches your life. Share your faith generously with those of another faith who question you about the Catholic way of life. Don't worry if you don't have answers. Knowledge is not what you have in your head. Rather, it's knowing where to go for answers.

- Take the initiative, and invite alienated Catholics to return to church. Encourage those who attend church only at Christmas and Easter to begin a more regular participation in parish life

Ordinarily we Catholics are not known for being evangelizers. In the past it was not the custom to talk about personal prayer life, religious viewpoints, or faith experiences. Today we believe that others can more readily know the Lord when we openly discuss our faith. Remember what the Lord said on this point:

> No one after lighting a lamp puts it under the bushel basket, but on the lampstand, and it gives light to all....let your light shine before others, so that they may see your good works. (Matthew 5:15-16)

Coming Into the Church the RCIA Way

What really is this RCIA? The acronym is becoming more familiar within the Church. It stands for Rite of Christian Initiation of Adults, the process by which adults ordinarily become full-fledged Catholics. It is primarily a *process*, but one that is filled with rites, ceremonies, and celebrations with prescribed words and focus. Each stage of the process is ritually celebrated, that is, recognized with special prayers and liturgical ceremony in the presence of the worshiping community.

The RCIA focuses on Christian initiation of adults through the reception of the sacraments of baptism, confirmation, and Eucharist, ordinarily celebrated in a single **liturgy** during the **Easter Vigil**. Teenagers who want to enter the Church, if they are mature enough, can join adults in the RCIA. Some parishes have the Rite of Christian Initiation for Children (RCIC), modified to accommodate children from age seven on.

The RCIA is not a new concept dreamed up by the **Second Vatican Council**. Rather it is the method by which people came into the Church in the first several centuries.

Why did Vatican II restore this ancient practice of the **catechumenate** in the form of the RCIA? When the bishops explored what *church* really means to us today, they found that, rather than being a static, lifeless institution, the Church is the People of God who journey through life bonded in a community of faith. The bishops of the world wisely decided to emphasize anew a concept that had been lost over time: church is a community of believers. Through sharing and praying together in the RCIA, both Catholics and **inquirers** find a way to live out their faith lives. The RCIA model works for this new understanding of Church because the training of new Catholic **Christians** goes hand-in-hand with the ongoing **formation** of the established community.

In the following pages we will explain in greater detail the basic concepts of the RCIA, the steps in the RCIA process, and practical ways to make the RCIA work in a parish.

Basic Concepts of the RCIA

Conversion is a process.

For a long time Bob's life had been aimless; making a living and earning money was all that mattered to him. Soon he became dissatisfied with his empty existence. He desired to become a better person. He sensed something essential was missing, but he hesitated to join any church. Soon he heard about an RCIA program at the local parish. The grace of God worked in his soul, and he became an avid RCIA inquirer. In time Bob became a full-fledged Catholic who had a deep personal relationship with Christ and who enthusiastically witnessed to the grace of true conversion.

Becoming Catholic is coming into a community of believers.

Jane's decision to join the parish RCIA brought more than she expected. She had been going to nondenominational services and Bible study, but they didn't satisfy. The **RCIA team** welcomed her, and Jane soon discovered that they not only cared for her spiritual growth but also joined with her in their own journey of faith. The team members, interested parishioners, and fellow inquirers shared how they prayed. They told how God acted in their lives and witnessed to Jesus' influence by authentic Christian caring. Jane soon realized she was not only becoming a Catholic but also was affiliated with a group of people who were true believers, living out their tradition.

The RCIA takes place in an experience of community.

Although Dan, a successful computer programmer, had no religious affiliation, he cherished integrity and honesty. His associates did not share his values, and Dan felt frustrated and alone in his ideals. Then a friend invited him to an RCIA session. The atmosphere of goodness and caring provided Dan with the spirit that was lacking in his workplace. Dan found the support of others with the same mind-set and values, although these people came from varying life experiences and backgrounds. Dan continued his journey of faith, anxiously awaiting the day he would belong to the parish as a committed Catholic.

The RCIA stages are celebrated in community with appropriate liturgical rites.

Father Joe, as the spiritual director of the RCIA, prepared diligently for the liturgical celebration of each stage in the RCIA. Each rite was a moving experience for the **catechumens**, **candidates**, team members, and the entire parish community. Father worked with the **music ministers** to prepare to creatively celebrate the occasion, and he always explained the significance of the rite to the worshiping community. He was proud to accompany the RCIA group to the cathedral for the **rite of election.** He introduced them to the bishop, so the catechumens and candidates could gain a sense of the universal nature of the Church. The Easter Vigil highlighted the liturgical year as the whole parish welcomed its newest members and celebrated the Lord's Resurrection.

Ann, a cradle Catholic and a pioneer in her parish RCIA, was asked by the pastor to oversee **breaking open the Word**. Although she was unfamiliar with this aspect of the RCIA, in which the catechumens are dismissed after the homily at Sunday Mass to delve deeper into the Scriptures, Ann willingly accepted. As weeks went by, she realized how superficial had been her own involvement in the Sunday readings.

The RCIA experience follows the flow of the liturgical seasons through a lectionary-based approach.

She came to understand more clearly how we relive Christ's life each year through the liturgical cycle and the Sunday readings. This experience not only gave her a deeper appreciation of the Scriptures but also demonstrated how our Catholic beliefs flow from the Scriptures. The catechumens acquired a greater sense of the connection of our Catholic beliefs when woven into the liturgical cycles. They also came to see how integral the Bible is to our Catholic faith. Ann's faith became more enriched in celebrating the paschal mysteries because it was coupled with a deeper understanding of the Scripture readings.

On Pentecost Sunday, Christ the King Parish was celebrating the coming of the Holy Spirit with a recognition of the newly baptized. Tom, a **neophyte**, was asked to speak to the congregation about his own journey of faith in the parish RCIA. He was proud of his two-thousand–year Christian legacy, rooted in the life and mission of Jesus. The witness Tom gave was ample proof of how the RCIA can change someone's life.

The RCIA process encourages authentic Catholicity.

From the time we were married I was too involved in my business to find time for the things of God and religion. But I saw how important religion was to my wife and children. When I decided to attend the RCIA, it was only to learn a little something about the Catholic faith that my wife and children professed.

But as I reflected on Matthew 16:15, "Who do you say I am?" I found true peace. I felt that Jesus was inviting me to share my wife's and children's faith. Since becoming a Catholic, I have shifted my life's priorities. Religion is now a part of my life. I find deep comfort in the Eucharist. As our family celebrates and receives the sacraments, we grow closer together

I know what the Lord expects of me as I follow the commandments and study the teachings of the Church. I feel a pride in being Catholic as I recite the Creed each Sunday with my family and parish. In coming into this community of faith, I sense the presence of Jesus. The Spirit is alive and at work here today. My newfound faith has also affected my work, for my coworkers say I am much easier to work with since I've gone through the RCIA. Just as the disciples did on the road to Emmaus, I am glad I said, "Lord, stay with me" (see Luke 24:13-º33a). And I am glad I heeded Jesus' invitation, "Come and see" (John 1:39).

The RCIA has prepared me well to be the kind of Catholic my wife and family had long prayed I would become. I thank all who have helped me find "the way, and the truth, and the life" (John 14:6). God bless you.

The RCIA: Reinstatement of Ancient Practice

This is just a sampling of what the RCIA does when it touches the lives of people in their spiritual quest. Wherever there is a vibrant RCIA program, the new Catholics (neophytes) are a challenge to seasoned Catholics to be the best they can be. Success of the program, for both new and seasoned Catholics, depends on the grace of God working through people and their witness.

Through the RCIA, parish communities can recapture the fervor of the first Christians, if parishes make use of the opportunities the RCIA presents. In observing how neophytes appreciate the faith, seasoned Catholics are encouraged to a deeper gratitude for the gift of faith in their own lives. The RCIA is the appropriate means to get in touch with our roots so we can incorporate into our present day the values of communal commitment to Christ and loving concern for each other, values that were lived out by the early Christians.

The RCIA—Rooted in History

Let us now consider how the catechumenate developed and why it is important to all of us that the RCIA be considered a vital aspect of parish life today.

The RCIA is an attempt to reinstate the original, meaningful way people came into the faith. In the first century, all that was required to be a Christian was to believe that Jesus is "the way, and the truth, and the life" (John 14:6). This belief called people to repent, receive baptism, and live the gospel message.

From the second to the fifth centuries, the Church articulated Christian beliefs and a way of life more completely. Early bishops' councils formulated the Creed as well as **dogmas** about Christ's true nature. More elaborate rituals gradually replaced earlier practices.

In A.D. 313, the Emperor Constantine proclaimed religious toleration through the Edict of Milan, ending official Roman persecution of Christianity. Christianity then became socially acceptable. So that people would not enter the Church to gain social prestige or through other unworthy motives, the Church required a period of formation (the catechumenate), followed by a dramatic single celebration during the Easter Vigil at which catechumens were initiated through the baptism of water and were sealed with the Spirit, which later became confirmation. They also partook of the Lord's Supper, which came to be called Eucharist.

As the Church expanded and infant baptism became more common, the formation process for adults was abbreviated and accommodated. Gradually the catechumenate as a formation process disappeared entirely. A person who desired to enter the Church received minimal individual instruction and formation. In the Middle Ages, a catechumen was merely required to know the rudiments of the faith—to recite the Creed and the Lord's Prayer. He or she was then brought into the Church in a private ceremony.

In response to the Reformation, the Council of Trent initiated more definitive ways of instilling the Catholic faith, one of which was the publication of catechisms containing the basics of faith. Converts were instructed individually and brought into the Church in private ceremonies. They were only required to memorize basic information, for example, the Ten Commandments, the Creed, the list of sacraments, basic prayers, and a confession formula. This manner of evangelization and formation lasted until the reforms of Vatican II.

One main objective of Vatican II was to return to the communal spirit of the early Church. The Council Fathers realized that, ever since the Reformation, people had been entering the Church in an individual and private way that emphasized head knowledge rather than spiritual formation. They decided that the ancient manner of accepting new members provided deeper formation and a more authentic understanding of the conversion process.

The restoration of the catechumenate as the ordinary way for adults to enter the Church was one of the most significant renewals made by Vatican II. The Rite of Christian Initiation of Adults was promulgated in 1972 by Pope Paul VI, and a provisional text was issued in 1974. In 1988 the American bishops mandated that all parishes in the U.S. use the RCIA as the process for new members to come into the Church, whether those new members were unbaptized or were coming from another Christian denomination. Although the format may vary from parish to parish, the RCIA follows a fixed pattern that is outlined and explained in the following section.

PART II

Structure and Format of the RCIA

The RCIA is a gradual process. Its format reflects all the elements of a growing relationship. Just as two people grow gradually toward establishing lasting bonds, the RCIA advances in stages from casual acquaintance to full commitment. Although the phases on the journey of faith cannot be compartmentalized, still there are distinguishing characteristics marking each step. The RCIA assists those coming into the Church in four distinct phases. Appropriate liturgical rites mark the transition to each phase.

The RCIA Process

PHASE ONE	Transition to PHASE TWO	PHASE TWO	Transition to PHASE THREE
Pre-Catechumenate, Inquiry, Pre-Evangelization People in this phase are inquirers.	***Rite of Acceptance into the Catechumenate*** Those not baptized are catechumens. Baptized Christians seeking full communion are candidates.	***Catechumenate*** Catechumens and candidates study the Catholic faith.	***Rite of Election*** Catechumens entering into the Purification and Enlightenment Phase are the elect.

PHASE THREE	Transition to PHASE FOUR	PHASE FOUR
Period of Purification Vigil and Enlightenment (Lenten Period) The elect engage in Lenten practice and celebrate the scrutinies with the community.	***The Easter Vigil Celebration*** Once initiated into the Church, the elect are neophytes.	***Mystagogy*** Neophytes claim a new role of service in the community. Pentecost marks the end of the RCIA process.

The RCIA Process Explained

The period of **inquiry** (**pre-evangelization** or pre-catechumenate) is the first phase on the journey of faith. It's a time of getting acquainted and feeling comfortable in the company of other seekers and Catholics. People who are thinking about whether they are called to the Catholic way of life are called *inquirers*.

Phase One: Period of Inquiry (Pre-Evangelization or Pre-Catechumenate Period)

The inquiry stage has no fixed structure or duration and is the most flexible in its format. Inquirers have time to share their life and faith stories. They receive answers to any questions they have, and any stereotypical ideas they may have about being Catholic are rounded out. The inquiry phase can take place in a parish setting or in informal gatherings in homes. Inquirers are invited to ask questions and to enter into **discernment** about whether the Catholic way of life is for them. The inquiry stage can last anywhere from several weeks to several years, depending on the individual situation. When inquirers decide to pursue the journey of faith into the catechumenate, they make a commitment through the **rite of acceptance**.

First Liturgical Rite: Acceptance into the Catechumenate

The rite of acceptance into the catechumenate is the celebration of the inquirers' intention to become Catholic and seriously continue the journey of faith toward baptism or full communion with the Church. This step is accepted by the Church and is the first liturgical rite that takes place in the presence of the community of faith, preferably at a Sunday liturgy.

Phase Two: The Catechumenate

The catechumenate phase marks the beginning of formal instructions in the faith. Prospective Catholics learn the basics of the faith and how to live the Catholic way of life in a process which is adapted to adult learning styles.

The content during the catechumenate phase is not textbook-oriented but is based on this fact: we have a God who loves us and who has revealed that love to us in Jesus. Catholic tradition is our means of knowing and understanding the life of Jesus. We are called to mirror that life in our way of living. So the catechumenate focuses on Jesus, his teachings, the Church, and the sacraments.

Unbaptized inquirers in the catechumenate are called *catechumens* and inquirers coming into the Church from another Christian denomination are called *candidates*. When catechumens and candidates enter the catechumenate, the community assigns to each one a **sponsor**, a member of the faith community who walks the faith journey with the catechumen or candidate in a one-on-one relationship.

The sponsor is a person with whom the candidate or catechumen feels free to share and pray. The sponsor enables the catechumen to discern more thoughtfully the decision to become a Catholic. Being a sponsor is a privilege and a serious responsibility. It is a ministry for someone who is willing to share personal faith and to assist another toward initiation or, in the case of candidates, toward committed Catholicism.

During the catechumenate, the catechumens and candidates take part in the Sunday Liturgy of the Word, although they do not participate in the Eucharist. They usually leave the assembly after the homily, with a blessing, because they will continue to explore the meaning of the Scripture readings (called *breaking open the Word*) while the rest of the community continues with the Liturgy of the Eucharist. This **dismissal** is a powerful sign and public witness to the community of faith of the sincerity and determination of those seeking to be Catholic. It shows that they are seriously pursuing their call and preparing to become full-fledged, committed Catholics.

The catechumens and candidates usually are accompanied by members of the RCIA team who serve as facilitators and leaders of the discussion about the Sunday readings. This lectionary-based approach to the catechumenate involves them in the spirit of the liturgical year and also enables them to relate the Scripture readings to their own lives.

The time spent as a catechumen or candidate varies with each person, but it is highly recommended that it last over a year. The catechumenate period allows for prospective Catholics to be married in church and to have a Christian burial.

Second Liturgical Rite: The Rite of Sending and Rite of Election

The catechumens and candidates conclude the catechumenate phase and enter the next phase of their faith journey, **Purification and Enlightenment**, through the **rite of sending** and the rite of election. Having discerned along with the RCIA team that they are called to the Catholic way of life, catechumens and candidates are officially called to the sacraments by the bishop or his representative in the rite of election.

Before the catechumens and candidates go to the cathedral for the rite of election, the parish celebrates this transition and sends them with a blessing through the rite of sending. This sending is celebrated at a Sunday liturgy before the rite of election, which ordinarily is celebrated on the First Sunday of **Lent**.

The rite of election is an elaborate and memorable event for those entering the Church. For the first time, they experience the Church not only on the parish level but also on the diocesan level, along with many others from the diocese who will be entering the Church at the upcoming Easter Vigil.

Catechumens coming into the Church are now **the**

elect. Having completed the period of formal instruction, they prepare more intensely through prayer experiences and spiritual renewal for the celebration of the paschal mystery and the reception of the sacraments of initiation. Catechumens enter their names into the Book of the Elect.

Phase Three: Lenten Period of Purification and Enlightenment

The third phase of the catechumenate ordinarily coincides with the Lenten season, a time of reconciliation, prayer, and spiritual renewal for the whole Church. Formal **catechesis** changes its focus. Those coming into the Church now turn their attention to interior reflection and conversion.

Lent is a time when the atmosphere of the regular sessions is more spiritual. The elect and candidates are introduced to various prayer forms through various prayer experiences. Since the Church emphasizes conversion during Lent, this is an appropriate time for those who are already baptized to receive the sacrament of reconciliation.

To impress upon the elect and the entire faith community the importance of self-discipline, the period of purification and enlightenment is also marked by the **scrutinies**. Held on the Third, Fourth, and Fifth Sundays of Lent, at the Sunday liturgy, the scrutinies include **exorcisms**, prayers for deliverance from evil and for the strength to be faithful to the gospel. The elect kneel in humility before the community, and the community prays for them. The intercessions focus on the spiritual needs of all, especially those of the elect.

Since those coming into the Church are preparing for full participation in the liturgy, they are presented with the two basic traditional prayers of the Church—the **Lord's Prayer** and the Creed. These prayers are often laminated or framed, and they become cherished mementos. The elect are also encouraged to pray these prayers regularly, and to memorize them so that when they attend the liturgy they can participate fully in their recitation.

The official rite recommends that the Lord's Prayer be presented sometime in Lent during a regular meeting session. This can be in conjunction with a discussion on the Lord's Prayer itself and a catechesis and sharing about prayer forms in general.

The Creed, the synthesis of our Christian beliefs, is presented sometime before the initiation at the Easter Vigil. It is recommended that the presentation of the Creed be made at a Sunday liturgy in the presence of the worshiping assembly.

An immediate preparation for the Easter Vigil takes place on Holy Saturday morning or at another appropriate time before the initiation. It is a period of retreat, spiritual reflection, and the celebration of preparatory rites—the **ephphatha** (see Mark 7:34-35) or opening of the senses, and the declaration of a baptismal name. If candidates have not availed themselves of the sacrament of reconciliation, the retreat is an appropriate time.

To allay any anxiety about what to do at the Easter Vigil, a practice session for the Easter Vigil initiation is recommended as part of the immediate preparation.

The celebration of the Lord's Resurrection and the initiation of new Catholics at the Easter Vigil is the climax and most important celebration of the liturgical year. Amid the symbolism and rituals of the Easter Vigil, the Church celebrates the paschal mystery—Christ's redemptive death and Resurrection.

The Easter Vigil is a liturgical celebration in which the

paradoxes of death and life, light and darkness, and sin and redemption are ritually observed. Because its themes are the paschal mystery and renewal in the life of Christ, the ceremony focuses on those who are being baptized or entering full communion with the Church.

The Easter Vigil, the longest and holiest ceremony of the entire Church year, encompasses all phases of the spiritual journey. It has four distinct parts:

1. The Service of Light, with the blessing of the Easter fire and lighting of the paschal candle, may take place outside the church proper.
2. The Liturgy of the Word, from the Hebrew Scriptures and the New Testament, recounts the story of our salvation.
3. The Liturgy of Baptism includes the baptismal ceremony, the profession of faith and renewal of baptismal promises of those who are already baptized, and confirmation.
4. The Liturgy of the Eucharist, during which those coming into the Church receive their First Communion.

Although new Catholics are received into the Church at the Easter Vigil, this is only the beginning of their lives as Catholics. The newly baptized are now called *neophytes*, a Greek term meaning "newly planted." But they and their newly Catholic companions continue their formation in the final stage of the process, which formally lasts until Pentecost.

Phase Four: Mystagogy

The new Catholics continue their journey of faith in a post-baptismal period called ***mystagogy***. Derived from a Greek word, *mystagogy* literally means "entering more deeply into the mystery." New Catholics use this time to reflect on the RCIA process, and the parish community helps them to begin participating actively in parish ministry.

During the regular meeting sessions, fellow parishioners introduce the new Catholics to specific ministries and show how they can become actively involved in parish life. The new Catholics examine how their own giftedness can best be used in parish ministry.

The Mystagogy usually lasts until Pentecost, when the new Catholics witness to their new-found faith in a celebratory liturgy. Although this marks the end of the formal RCIA process, they are encouraged to continue to be part of the RCIA, now as full-fledged Catholics.

Celebration of the Paschal Mystery—Christian Initiation

Although the RCIA may come to an end for one group, the RCIA ideally is a continuous process in which there are always people at various stages. This way of conducting the program requires more time, effort, and personnel because there may be such a great variety of individual circumstances. But the RCIA exists for the benefit of the inquirers. At times the program may need to be adjusted to meet special needs.

Ruth had never had any religious affiliation. But when her husband, Dick, a lapsed Catholic, became terminally ill, she realized how important religion was in her life. She applied and was accepted into the RCIA. But because of the constant care Dick required, she was unable to attend the sessions. The RCIA coordinator kept Ruth abreast of the process, and in addition, RCIA team members visited Ruth regularly.

On Palm Sunday, Ruth called the parish to say that Dick probably would not live until Easter. But he had asked to make his peace with the Church, and he wanted to have the joy of seeing Ruth become a Catholic. The pastor and the team members decided to hold an anticipated celebration in the home. At that celebration, Dick made a fervent confession and was reconciled to the Church. He received the sacrament of anointing of the sick, and Father validated their marriage. Ruth was baptized, confirmed, and received her First Communion. The Eucharist Dick received was his last, for he died on Good Friday. Six sacraments of the Church at once! What a celebration it was!

PART III

Roles and Ministries in the RCIA

Those who are inquiring about or seeking full communion with the Catholic Church are the raw material of the RCIA. As they progress in their journey of faith they are called various names—inquirers, catechumens or candidates, the elect, and neophytes. The RCIA is designed specifically for them. Without them, there is no RCIA. But when there is an operative RCIA, there is also a need for people to carry out a variety of functions to support the process.

Although the official Rite of Christian Initiation of Adults does not call for an RCIA team, the very structure and mode of operation of the RCIA implicitly demands the formation of an RCIA team. Team roles ideally are filled by different persons if an RCIA team is blessed with many members. The roles and functions of team members may also overlap. Since the RCIA is highly flexible, there may be other roles that can be creatively introduced. The following roles are basic to generating an effective RCIA in a parish.

- RCIA COORDINATOR OR DIRECTOR — organizes the RCIA and delegates tasks to various team members. The coordinator is usually the first contact person when an inquirer asks about joining the RCIA. This ideally would be a person with a professional degree in religious education or theology.

- SPIRITUAL DIRECTOR — oversees spiritual growth and gives direction. The spiritual director is ordinarily a priest or a pastoral associate who examines the participants to determine their readiness for the various steps, especially to help them prepare for the sacrament of reconciliation without distress or worry.

- CATECHIST — instructs in the formal catechesis. The catechist does not necessarily have to be someone with a teaching or theology degree but should be someone who is knowledgeable enough to instruct and answer questions about the Catholic faith.

- SPONSOR — supports and encourages the one seeking membership in the Church. A sponsor is by far the most important person for an individual coming into the Church. In this one-on-one relationship with the one seeking membership, the sponsor becomes mentor, guide, and confidante. Therefore, the one who assumes the role of sponsor receives a sacred trust. The sponsor accompanies the prospective Catholic on the journey of faith, answers questions, and is present at the RCIA sessions.

- GODPARENT — formally witnesses the reception of the sacraments of baptism and confirmation. The catechumen or candidate chooses a practicing Catholic to be godparent. Although the roles of sponsor and godparent can be distinct, one person can ideally act in both roles for the catechumen or candidate.

- LITURGY PLANNER — coordinates the liturgy for the specific rites. The liturgy planner informs the presider, music minister, lector, and commentator about plans for any upcoming rituals that will be taking place during a Sunday liturgy.

- HOSPITALITY PERSONNEL — welcome and greet the participants. Although the hospitality ministry belongs to everyone, specifically assigned people act as hosts. They arrange the social aspects of the RCIA.

- PHYSICAL ENVIRONMENT OVERSEERS — set up the meeting room, provide TV and VCR, and clean up. These tasks, too, should be shared by all, but there are some in the group who are more adept at the physical aspects than others. It always is helpful to have a mechanically knowledgeable person on the team, someone who can oversee the temperature, arrange furniture, and provide necessary muscle power.

- INTERESTED OBSERVERS — attend sessions, although they may not have any specific role or contribution. The RCIA is primarily geared to prospective Catholics and is not a substitute for adult education. But parishioners may find that their attendance at the RCIA enriches their faith, supports the inquirers, and provides updated information, especially regarding changes in the Church.

- PRAYER PARTNERS — support catechumens and candidates by prayer but do not otherwise participate. This is an ideal ministry for the elderly and homebound, but any parishioner can share in this important task. A coordinator can assign prayer partners.

- PLANNER AND DIRECTOR OF PRAYER EXPERIENCES — selects and sets up the prayer experiences. One of the most important facets of the RCIA is prayer. Not only do participants need to be taught about prayer, but they also need to pray. The different prayer forms that they experience in the RCIA will help to form their own unique spirituality and prayer life.

- RECORD KEEPER — gathers pertinent personal information, especially important for the sacramental records. Since the participants are preparing to enter the Church, accurate attendance records are necessary. In the beginning it is also necessary to ascertain whether a marriage concern needs to be addressed, especially regarding filing for an **annulment**.

- PUBLIC RELATIONS PERSONNEL — make known and advertise the RCIA. Like any successful program, the RCIA must be publicized if it is to flourish in a parish. The RCIA is not an isolated segment of parishioners attending closed sessions but is a responsibility of the entire community of faith.

- COMMUNICATIONS DIRECTOR — handles bulletin announcements, sends out letters about meeting dates and other communications. Communication lapses are a major obstacle to any program. The communications director must constantly be aware of who is to be informed about RCIA happenings.

- RESOURCE DIRECTOR — orders books and materials and sets up a library for the RCIA. Since not all the pertinent material can be handled in the RCIA sessions, adequate supplementary reading should be available. Handouts help to clarify many topics. The resource director also keeps abreast of new publications about the RCIA and related subjects.

The Qualities of an RCIA Team Member

Who ideally makes up the RCIA core team, those who work directly with participants in the RCIA process? Although an individual may not possess all of the following characteristics, these qualities are present in the core team as a whole. Usually a team member has several strengths to contribute to the RCIA process.

Practicing Catholic

The team member need not be highly educated but must be a person who loves the faith and is willing to help others to develop a relationship with Christ. An RCIA team member is an active parishioner and readily shares personal experiences of God.

Spiritually Mature

An ideal team member is one who is open to all legitimate forms of spirituality, an ordinary Catholic who can distinguish between what is basic and what is optional in the Catholic faith. A team member must not foist a favorite devotion or form of spirituality on inquirers.

A person of prayer and principles, the team member is part of a group and strives to build an atmosphere of community and support. *Team Oriented*

Although a team member may not always agree with what goes on in the Church, being negative or cynical hampers a member's ability to share the good news. RCIA team members realize that the Church is human but avoid instilling negative notions in newcomers. *Loyal*

An RCIA team member is very much aware that we are all lifelong learners and searchers. Even though the team member may be a cradle Catholic, no one has all the answers. But a team member knows where to begin looking for answers. *Humble*

Each person's spiritual journey requires ongoing conversion. A team member's life reflects the saying, "Please be patient. God isn't finished with me yet." *Patient*

Since the RCIA is geared to adult learners, the team member needs to be aware of the process of adult learning. The ultimate RCIA aim is the formation of good Catholics who have a personal relationship with the Lord and who cherish the legacy of the Catholic faith. Not everything can be taught in the RCIA. The spirit of the Catholic way of life needs to be *caught*. It is adult-centered learning, respectful of the manner in which adults learn, through sharing and the expression of opinion. *Respectful*

When an RCIA team member appreciates the Lectionary method of catechesis and is an ardent lover of the Scriptures, the theology falls into place through the *Prayerful and Knowledgeable* discussions. Doctrine springs naturally out of the Scriptures and the liturgical cycles.

A prospective team member may feel inadequate when considering the above characteristics. However, the RCIA is one form of the conversion process, to which all Christians are called. That person has great potential as an RCIA team member who has a respect for the Catholic faith, strives to build community, and has an awareness that each person's faith grows according to God's grace. The RCIA team is not composed of canonization candidates but of ordinary pilgrims on the journey of faith.

PART IV

How to Build a Parish RCIA Program

Core Concepts

When Vatican II reinstated the catechumenate as the norm for entrance into the Church, the Council Fathers realized that Catholics needed to readjust their understanding of the following basic theological concepts.

1. Understanding of *Church*

For Catholics brought up before Vatican II, *church* meant being Catholic, going to Mass, receiving the sacraments, and obeying the laws of God and of the Church.

According to Vatican II, *church* is the People of God bringing good news into the world, making Christ's peace known. The RCIA demonstrates in its whole process this community aspect of Church. To be Catholic is to join with others in a community of faith, a People of God, who together worship, pray, share, and are present for each other in time of need. This is an entirely new understanding of what it means to be Church. Being Catholic in the post-Vatican II era refers not only to attending Sunday Mass but also to joining with others in a witness to Christ's presence in the world.

2. Understanding of conversion

Catholics also need to rethink their notion of conversion. In years gone by, conversion had one meaning for Catholics—to become Catholic or to change from one faith to another. People attuned to the RCIA process are becoming more aware of the true meaning of conversion—the inner change of an individual's whole being, attitude, and relationships with God, others, and self. Conversion involves a commitment to a Catholic way of life and to Christian ideals, not just as a solo journey but brought about by a communal effort. Conversion means building up the body of Christ on all levels, starting with the self and then reaching out to others. Conversion is for everyone, not just prospective Catholics. We all are on a lifelong journey of conversion.

3. Understanding the difference between knowing the faith and living the faith

When a parish dons an authentic RCIA mentality, it automatically will accommodate its notion of what it means to know the faith. There is a distinction between knowing about the faith and experiencing the faith through the example and witness of others. The RCIA process accentuates the example and witness aspect of the faith and deemphasizes merely knowing facts about the Church. Although it is necessary to know certain basics, the RCIA process takes a holistic view of knowledge, an experiential knowledge that encompasses a person's whole being. Factual and head knowledge must be superceded by spiritual formation and attitude. Dead facts must come alive with a spirit of witness. An authentic RCIA makes a clear distinction between living our faith and knowing about the faith.

4. Distinction between the essentials and optional personal devotions and practices

Another important notion to be clarified in any RCIA process is the distinction between the essentials of the Catholic faith and optional personal devotions and prayers. Sometimes well-intentioned Catholics introduce a devotional practice to an unsuspecting catechumen without making clear that the devotion is optional and not a basic belief. Although many practices are steeped in long traditions and are popular with Catholics, newcomers need to be told the difference so they can choose the personal prayers and devotions they prefer.

5. Distinction between those unbaptized, those baptized coming from another Christian denomination, and uncatechized Catholics

Although the RCIA process is primarily directed to the unbaptized, there are two other groups who may make up RCIA participants—properly baptized persons converting from another Christian denomination and properly baptized but uncatechized Catholics (Catholics baptized as infants who have not grown up practicing the faith). These two groups are not rebaptized but instead participate in a penitential rite, which is usually held on the Second Sunday of Lent. During the RCIA process, they prepare to receive any other sacraments they have not as yet received, and they participate in the catechesis.

Within the process, special attention is given to the

unbaptized. They alone are called catechumens. They alone sign the Book of the Elect at the cathedral and are the primary subject of the Lenten scrutinies.

Pastoral Issues

Since the RCIA is not just another program but is a vital factor in parish renewal, the whole parish needs to know about the process. Everyone must be involved, especially by creating a welcoming atmosphere and by celebrating the rites meaningfully. Some parishioners serve by being directly involved in the program.

1. Educating the community of faith about the nature of the RCIA

The celebration of the various rites during liturgy are teachable moments for the whole worshiping community. It is an ideal time to catechize the community of faith about the RCIA process and about everyone's challenge to be faithful to their baptismal commitment. The celebration of the rites also provides an excellent setting for an explanation of what the rites signify and to impress on the parishioners their role as prayerful supporters of the catechumens.

2. Getting the parish RCIA off the ground

The basic ingredient of any parish RCIA is a core group of people who practice the faith and are willing to invest time and talent in helping others on their faith journey. This core group, made up of a cross-section of the parish community, has what it takes to bring an active RCIA to life. A parish may have the most up-to-date facilities, a hefty budget, and an interested group of inquirers. But if on the one hand it lacks the movers and shakers of the process, little will be accomplished. On the other hand, if all a parish has are a few dedicated and involved parishioners, that parish probably will succeed in its RCIA attempts. A core group is the lifeline and spirit of the RCIA.

3. Considering marriage cases and the annulment process

Shortly after inquirers appear on the scene, the RCIA coordinator should determine if there are any marriage issues that need to be addressed. Is the inquirer married? Is it a valid marriage? Has the inquirer been previously married? Has the inquirer been divorced? The intention is not to pry but to acquire information necessary for the inquirer to continue in the process of becoming Catholic. An inquirer may need to apply for an annulment or to have an existing marriage validated. Getting this information early can prevent embarrassing situations later.

4. Demonstrating the importance of sacramental preparation programs to parents

The RCIA process shows how important it is to prepare spiritually to receive the sacraments. This can be a witness to parents whose children are preparing for the sacraments. Because parents and family are the first church, parents provide their children with a powerful example of what it means to be Catholic. Vatican II mandated sacramental preparation programs for parents of children who will be receiving sacraments so that the parents can themselves be evangelized, educated, and updated in the thinking of the Church today.

5. Solidifying a parish identity

One reason people enter the Church is to belong to a community of faith. This sense of belonging to a particular worshiping family is what often draws people to the Catholic way of life. The importance of parish identity is an issue to be seriously addressed during the catechumenate. People seeking membership in the Church are not coming just to be able to receive the sacraments. Authentic Catholics are conscious of the social dimension of being Catholic, of belonging to a definite local church through which they put the faith into practice. Catholics who attend Mass at a different church each Sunday so as not to get involved in a parish are Catholics in name only.

RCIA Terms

Since the RCIA is a comparatively new concept in the modern church, terms that relate to the RCIA process may not be familiar to the ordinary Catholic. Often these words have been derived from Latin or Greek and have not been part of a Catholic's vocabulary, especially for those educated before Vatican II. The terms related to the RCIA are listed below so that they can become Catholic household words.

- ANNULMENT — a declaration issued by Church authority that a sacramental marriage never existed.

- BREAKING OPEN THE WORD — reflecting on the Scriptures. Beginning at the catechumenate stage, those coming into the church attend the Liturgy of the Word. After the homily they are dismissed to break open the Word, discussing the passages and how they apply to their lives.

- CANDIDATE — one baptized in another denomination who wishes to become Catholic. Such a person is called a candidate during the catechumenate.

- CATECHESIS — instruction in the Catholic faith.

- CATECHIST — anyone (clergy, religious, or lay person) who instructs others in Catholicism.

- CATECHUMEN — one never baptized who wishes to become Catholic. Such a person is called a catechumen during the catechumenate.

- CATECHUMENATE — the entire RCIA process. More specifically, the catechumenate is the period of formal instruction, the second phase of RCIA.

- CHRISTIANS — the baptized who base their religious faith on the life and teachings of Jesus, specifically, Catholics, the Orthodox, and Protestants.

- COMMUNITY OF FAITH (FAITH COMMUNITY) — Christians in a local parish assembly united by common beliefs, worship, and daily living of gospel values.

- CONVERSION — change of mind, heart, and spirit resulting in growth in personal faith and improvement in relationships with God, others, and self.

- DISCERNMENT — prayerful reflection with the aid of the Holy Spirit to help a person make responsible decisions according to God's will.

- DISMISSAL — blessing given to catechumens and candidates, who leave the assembly after the Sunday Liturgy of the Word and homily to reflect more deeply on the Scripture readings.

- DOGMAS — Catholic teachings officially proclaimed as truths of faith.

- EASTER VIGIL — Holy Saturday evening celebration of the Resurrection, including solemn initiation of new members into the Church.

- ELECT, THE — those preparing for full initiation into the Church. Catechumens are called the elect after the rite of election during Lent.

- ENLIGHTENMENT, (PURIFICATION AND) — Lenten period of spiritual preparation, penance, and renewal before Christian initiation.

- EPHPHATHA — literally, "be opened." This blessing of the ears and mouths of the elect, so that they may hear the Word of God and profess it, is given in the preparatory rite on Holy Saturday or at the retreat.

- EVANGELIZATION — the carrying out of the Lord's mandate to "go…and make disciples of all nations" (Matthew 28:19). It is the sharing of one's faith and spreading the good news of Jesus Christ.

- EXORCISMS — ritual prayers of delivery from sin, evil, and evil influences; part of the scrutinies, which are celebrated on the Third, Fourth, and Fifth Sundays of Lent.

- FAITH-SHARING — sharing with others one's spirituality and relationship with the Lord.

- FORMATION — process of shaping a person's mature spirituality; specifically applied to the whole RCIA process, which forms new Catholics.

- GODPARENT — practicing Catholic chosen to be official witness at baptism.

- INITIATION — rites and ceremonies by which one becomes a member of a religious group. In the RCIA process, the sacraments of initiation are baptism, confirmation, and Eucharist.

- INQUIRERS — people who express interest in learning about the Catholic faith during the pre-evangelization phase of the RCIA.

- INQUIRY — initial phase of the RCIA process, pre-evangelization or pre-catechumenate.

- LENT — the forty-day period of preparation and penance before Easter. In the RCIA, Lent is called the period of Purification and Enlightenment.

- LITURGY — rites and ceremonies that comprise the Church's official public worship of God—the Mass, the Liturgy of the Hours, and the sacraments.

- LORD'S PRAYER — a basic prayer tradition of the Church, first taught by Jesus when the disciples said, "Lord, teach us to pray" (see Luke 11:1-4). A formal presentation of the Lord's Prayer and catechesis on prayer is part of the Lenten experience.

- MINISTRY — any church-related activity that serves the physical, emotional, and spiritual needs of the people of God.

- MYSTAGOGY — period after Easter when new Catholics learn more about the Church and its ministries. *Mystagogy* is a Greek word that means *entering more deeply into the mysteries.*

- NEOPHYTE — newly baptized Catholic, one brought into full communion with the Church. *Neophyte* is from the Greek meaning *newly planted.*

- PRE-EVANGELIZATION — first phase of the entire RCIA process. It is preparatory and is also called the *inquiry stage* or the *pre-catechumenate.*

- PURIFICATION AND ENLIGHTENMENT — third phase of the RCIA process, occurring during Lent.

- RCIA (RITE OF CHRISTIAN INITIATION OF ADULTS) — name given to the entire catechumenate.

- RCIA TEAM — group of people who guide the RCIA and are responsible for its success in a parish. As representatives of the whole parish, the team is a vital, necessary component of the RCIA.

- RCIC (RITE OF CHRISTIAN INITIATION OF CHILDREN) — a modification of the rite for adults, it is geared to the needs and understanding of children.

- RITE — the specific way Catholic liturgy is carried out; the words and ceremonies prescribed for liturgy or sacraments; in the RCIA process of the Latin or Roman Rite, the rites are liturgical ceremonies celebrated in the presence of the worshiping assembly. They mark the beginning of each stage of the RCIA process. There are four distinct RCIA rites. (See below.)

  RITE OF ACCEPTANCE — the rite that celebrates the beginning of the catechumenate stage.

  RITE OF ELECTION — a rite, usually celebrated on the First Sunday of Lent, which begins the Purification and Enlightenment phase of intense spiritual preparation. The rite of election is usually celebrated with the bishop at the cathedral.

  RITE OF INITIATION — the primary goal of the RCIA process. It is celebrated with great solemnity at the Easter Vigil, held after sundown on Holy Saturday evening. The elect become full-fledged Catholics and receive the sacraments of initiation—baptism, confirmation, and Eucharist.

  RITE OF SENDING — a rite held in the parish to send forth the catechumens to the bishop for the rite of election, on the First Sunday of Lent.

- SCRUTINIES — rituals that mark the final preparation of catechumens to receive the sacraments of initiation; celebrated during the Mass of the Third, Fourth, and Fifth Sundays of Lent.

- SECOND VATICAN COUNCIL (VATICAN II) — meetings of the pope with all the world's bishops (1962-1965); an update and renewal of the Church, adjusting its practices and laws to modern times.

- SPONSOR — companion and support person for a candidate or catechumen.

- WITNESS — the proclamation of faith in Jesus and the Church by words and actions; the public testimony given by participants in the RCIA.

Conclusion

The RCIA—Sign of a Church That Is Fully Alive

The main concern of the pastor of a parish is the life and spirituality of the people, although he also is responsible for the liturgical environment and upkeep of the physical plant. However, the pastor cannot and should not do it alone. The people of the parish are the soul and spirit of the local Church. The following tale demonstrates this truth in a dramatic way.

The Parable of the Dead Church

Once upon a time a pastor was disgruntled with the apathy and lack of cooperation of his congregation. So he decided to take drastic measures. He had placards posted all over town that read: ***The church at Main and Pine Streets has died. You are all invited to come to its funeral service this Sunday evening at 7 p.m. to give the church a fitting farewell.***

Needless to say, the church was packed to overflowing because the whole town wanted to see what was going on. As people entered, they noticed that the church had all the trappings of a wake. Soft organ music played doleful tunes. The local funeral director acted as usher and host. Flowers blanketed the sanctuary. There was even an open coffin in the center aisle.

The pastor proceeded to tell the assembly of the merits of the dead church. Then he invited each person present to give the church a personal farewell, to approach the casket individually and to pay their last respects. As you can imagine, everyone was anxious to peer into the coffin. As they did so, each one was taken aback. The pastor had placed a life-sized mirror in the coffin, so that each person saw his or her own image. From then on the congregation was cooperative and alive in the spirit.

In parishes where there is life, the RCIA will thrive. Where the evangelization spirit is lacking, where there are no new members, the fate of the parish may be in jeopardy.

When integrated into parish life, the RCIA can be an effective catalyst in the renewal and spiritual growth of the entire faith community. The RCIA can serve also as a valuable basis for continuing adult formation. An operative RCIA is one of the vital signs—the spiritual temperature—of a vibrant parish.

When the RCIA has vitality, the parish as a whole is a living sign of Christ's continuing presence in the world. The RCIA reflects Vatican II's vision of what the Church can be in our age—a continuation of the mission of Jesus. The parish faith community hands on the tradition through the RCIA. Thus the parish family fulfills its baptismal mission. A vibrant RCIA in a parish takes seriously Christ's admonition, "You received without payment; give without payment" (Matthew 10:8).

Just as we cherish a treasured family heirloom and pass it from generation to generation, so the Catholic faith heritage is passed on through a dynamic and energetic RCIA. The ultimate RCIA goal, to be Eucharist for the world, carries out Vatican II's vision of what the Church is in our day—the manifestation of Christ's presence and grace at work in the world.